# PEEK-A-BOO CAKES

## 28 FUN CAKES WITH A SURPRISE INSIDE!

# JOANNA FARROW

## PHOTOGRAPHS BY LIS PARSONS

An Hachette UK Company
www.hachette.co.uk

First published in Great Britain in 2014 by Spruce,
a division of Octopus Publishing Group Ltd,
Endeavour House, 189 Shaftesbury Avenue,
London, WC2H 8JY
www.octopusbooks.co.uk
www.octopusbooksusa.com

Distributed in the USA by Hachette Book Group USA
237 Park Avenue, New York, NY 10017, USA

Distributed in Canada by Canadian Manda Group
165 Dufferin Street, Toronto, Ontario, Canada, M6K 3H6

ISBN 978-1-84601-477-2

A CIP catalogue record for this book is available from the
British Library.

Printed and bound in China.

10 9 8 7 6 5 4 3 2 1

Consultant Publisher: Sarah Ford
Senior Editor: Leanne Bryan
Designer: Eoghan O'Brien
Photographer: Lis Parsons
Food Stylist: Joanna Farrow
Production Controller: Sarah Connelly

# CONTENTS

# INTRODUCTION

Peek-a-boo cakes are the latest trend in baking. Cakes that look delicious but minimally decorated are sliced to reveal a feast of color, shapes, and fun that will entertain and delight. Some of the cakes are easy to make while others require more creative input, patience, and commitment.

# FROSTING RECIPES

The quantities for all these delicious frostings and cake toppings are sufficient to sandwich cake layers together and provide a simple covering that hides the treat inside!

MACARON LAYER CAKE (page 58)

## VANILLA BUTTERCREAM

1¾ sticks (200 g) unsalted butter, softened
2¼ cups (300 g) confectioners' sugar
1 tablespoon vanilla extract
1 tablespoon boiling water

Put the butter, confectioners' sugar, and vanilla extract in a large bowl and beat with a wooden spoon or an electric hand beater until smooth. Add the water and beat again until pale and creamy.

### VARIATIONS:

For lemon buttercream: add 4 tablespoons lemon juice instead of the vanilla extract and water. For chocolate buttercream: add ½ cup (50 g) unsweetened cocoa powder and an extra 2 tablespoons boiling water.

## COCONUT FROSTING

Scant ½ cup (100 ml) heavy cream
3 oz (75 g) creamed coconut, chopped if firm
4 teaspoons lemon or lime juice
3½ cups (500 g) confectioners' sugar

Put the cream and creamed coconut in a small saucepan and heat gently until the coconut has melted.

Tip into a large bowl and stir in the lemon or lime juice. Gradually beat in the confectioners' sugar with a wooden spoon or an electric hand beater until the consistency is thick and smooth.

## CREAM CHEESE FROSTING

1¾ cups (400 g) full-fat cream
  cheese
7 tablespoons (100 g) unsalted
  butter, softened
2 teaspoons lemon juice
Generous ²/3 cup (100 g)
  confectioners' sugar

Beat the cream cheese and butter
together in a large bowl with a
wooden spoon or an electric hand
beater until evenly mixed. Stir in
the lemon juice.

Add the confectioners' sugar
and beat the frosting again until
smooth and creamy.

NEAPOLITAN SURPRISE CAKE (pages 62-3)

## MERINGUE FROSTING

4 large egg whites
½ teaspoon cream of tartar
Generous 1¹/3 cups (200 g)
  confectioners' sugar

Put the egg whites, cream of
tartar, and confectioners' sugar
in a large heatproof bowl and rest
the bowl over a saucepan of gently
simmering water. Beat with a
wooden spoon or an electric hand
beater until softly peaking.

Remove from the heat and beat
for another 3–5 minutes until
thick and glossy.

### VARIATION:

For chocolate meringue frosting:
add ²/3 cup (75 g) sifted
unsweetened cocoa powder to
the bowl and make as above.

## DARK CHOCOLATE GANACHE

1 ²/3 cups (400 ml) heavy cream
4 tablespoons superfine sugar
14 oz (400 g) semisweet chocolate,
  chopped

Heat half the cream in a small
saucepan with the sugar until hot
and bubbling around the edges
but not boiling.

Pour over the chocolate in a large
bowl and stir frequently until the
chocolate has melted. Stir in the
remaining cream and chill until
the mixture is thick enough to hold
its shape before using.

### VARIATION:

For white chocolate
ganache: make the recipe
as above, omitting the
sugar and using white
chocolate instead of
the semisweet. If the
ganache doesn't
thicken on chilling,
beat lightly with an
electric hand
beater. (Don't
overbeat it or
the ganache will
turn granular.)

# USEFUL TECHNIQUES AND TIPS

### PASTRY BAGS

Reusable nylon pastry bags, available from cake-decorating shops or cook shops, can be fitted with a piping tip for piping cake mixtures and frostings. Alternatively use disposable paper or plastic pastry bags (which can be bought in various sizes) or make your own (see below). For piping frostings when using disposable or homemade pastry bags, simply snip off the tip and fit with a piping tip that gives a more precise finish. For piping cake mixtures that don't require perfect piping, simply snip off the tip.

STRAWBERRY CHEESE CAKE (pages 44–5)

To make a paper pastry bag, cut out a 15-inch/38-cm square (for a large bag) or a 10-inch/25-cm square (for a small bag) from parchment paper and fold diagonally in half, creasing well. Cut the paper in half to create two triangles. Hold one triangle by the central point then take the left-hand point and bend it round to meet the central point, creating a cone shape. Now, holding these two points together, take the right-hand point and wrap it right round the cone to meet the other two points. Fold the points over several times to hold the cone in shape. Snip off the tip to insert a piping tip before filling the cone, or snip off the tip once the cone is filled if you are piping without a tip.

Alternatively, plastic food bags can be used for piping cake mixtures or frostings. Fill the bag, pressing the mixture into one corner with a spoon. Twist the bag to create a pastry bag shape and snip off the tip. Food bags do not work with piping tips so cannot be used for intricate piping.

### USING FOOD COLORINGS

Food colorings are available in liquid, gel, or paste forms and can all be used in cake mixtures and frostings. Generally the pastes give a stronger, more vibrant color, and are particularly good for coloring without softening the ingredients you are working them into, such as marzipan.

When coloring a frosting, beat the coloring in with a wooden spoon until evenly distributed. When coloring cake mixtures—particularly when using a thick paste—work the color into a small amount of the mixture to make sure it is evenly distributed before stirring the colored mixture into the main batch. To do this, put a heaping tablespoon of the cake mixture into a bowl and add the coloring. Use the back of a spoon to work the color into the mix. Once it is evenly colored, add it to the rest of the cake mixture and stir it in until just combined. If the color is not dense enough, work a little more color into another tablespoonful of mixture as above.

# HOW TO LINE A...

## LAYER PAN

Draw around the pan on a sheet of wax paper with a sharp pencil (stack two or three layers of paper depending on how many cake layers you are baking). Cut out the circle(s) with a pair of scissors. Grease the base and side of the pan with softened butter and fit the paper in the base. Grease the paper. Put a little flour in the pan and tip it around the side, tilting the pan until the side is coated. Tip out the excess.

## ROUND CAKE PAN

Draw around the pan on a sheet of wax paper and cut out the circle. Grease the base and side of the pan with softened butter. Cut out strips of paper that are slightly wider than the height of the pan. Fold over a ¾-inch (1.5-cm) lip along one long edge of the paper and snip it at intervals to the fold. Fit the paper around the side of the pan so the snipped edge sits on the base. Press the circle into the base. Grease the paper.

## SQUARE CAKE PAN

Use the same technique as for a round pan but snip the strip at the corners only.

## LOAF PAN

Grease the base and sides of the pan with softened butter. Cut a wide strip of wax paper that is long enough to cover the base and long sides of the pan and overhang the sides slightly. Press the strip into the pan and grease the paper.

## SHALLOW BAKING OR ROASTING PAN

Grease the base and sides of the pan with softened butter. Cut out a rectangle of wax paper that is at least 4 inches (10 cm) longer and wider than the size of the pan. Press the paper into the pan, folding it at the corners to fit. Grease the paper.

## USING FOOD CANS

Food cans are great for baking very small cakes. Line as for a round cake pan. If you are using a ring-pull can, there may be a metal lip around the top of the can. Remove this with a can opener, working carefully as the edge may be sharp.

## SLICING CAKES

Cakes are less crumbly and slice more cleanly a day after they are baked when the texture has firmed up. Try to bake the cake a day in advance if you are making a cake that needs to be sliced into shapes

CHOCOLATE, FRUIT, AND NUT CAKE (page 42)

SPRINKLE SPECKLED CAKE (page 24)

or layers, or you are cutting shapes from the cake using a metal cutter.

## WHAT TO DO WITH LEFTOVER CAKE

Most of the cakes are shaped or cut leaving some excess cake or cake trimmings. Don't waste these as cake freezes so well. Cut into pieces for using in trifles or for crumbling up and using as the sponge base for cake pops.

SERVES 12
PREPARATION AND DECORATING TIME
ABOUT 1 HOUR, PLUS COOLING

3⅛ sticks (350 g) slightly salted butter, softened, plus extra for greasing

2¾ cups (350 g) self-rising flour, plus extra for dusting

1⅔ cups (350 g) superfine sugar

Finely grated zest of 3 lemons, plus 3 tablespoons juice

6 large eggs

TO DECORATE

1 quantity Lemon Buttercream (see page 4)

1 lb (500 g) jelly beans, or other small candies of your choice

# JELLY BEAN SURPRISE CAKE

## TO MAKE THE CAKE

Preheat the oven to 350°F (180°C). Grease and base-line 2 × 7-inch (18-cm) round layer pans and dust the sides with flour (see page 7). Put the butter, sugar, lemon zest and juice, flour, and eggs in a large bowl and beat with an electric hand beater until the mixture is pale and creamy. Spoon one-quarter of the mixture (about 11½ oz/350 g) into one pan and the same quantity into the other pan. Level the surfaces and bake for 25 minutes or until just firm to the touch. Loosen the edges of the cakes with a knife and transfer to a cooling rack to cool. Wash the layer pans and grease and re-line them. Bake the remaining mixture in the same way. Turn each of the cakes out to cool then peel away the lining paper.

Cut out the centers of 2 of the cake layers using a 3½-inch (9-cm) round metal cutter. If you don't have a cutter, position a small bowl or container on the sponges and cut around it with a knife, keeping the knife vertical. Lift out the centers. (Make a mini cake with these, sandwiching with jelly or buttercream and dusting with confectioners' sugar, or freeze for another time—see page 7.)

## TO DECORATE

Place one of the whole cakes on a plate and use a spatula to spread the edges and top with a little lemon buttercream. Position one of the ring cakes on top. Spread the edges and top of this with buttercream and position the second ring cake on top of it. Tip the jelly beans or candies into the cavity until it is completely filled. Spread the cake edges and top with more buttercream and position the remaining cake on top.

Spread a thin layer of buttercream around the sides of the top cake to seal in the crumbs. Spread the remaining buttercream over the top and sides of the cake in an even layer.

2 sticks (225 g) slightly
   salted butter, softened,
   plus extra for greasing

11 oz (300 g) marzipan

2½ cups (300 g) self-rising
   flour, plus extra for
   dusting

Blue, pink, green, and lilac
   paste food colorings

Generous ¾ cup (175 g)
   superfine sugar

3 large eggs, beaten

1 teaspoon almond extract

1 cup (100 g) ground
   almonds

2 tablespoons whole milk

TO DECORATE

4 tablespoons apricot jelly

lilac paste food coloring

1 lb 12 oz (800 g) marzipan

Confectioners' sugar, for
   dusting

4 ft (1.2 m) colored ribbon,
   about 1 inch (2.5 cm) wide

# MARZIPAN RAINBOW CAKE

TO MAKE THE CAKE

Preheat the oven to 325°F (160°C). Grease and line the base and side of
a 7-inch (18-cm) round, deep cake pan (see page 7). Divide the marzipan
into 4 × 2¾-oz (75-g) pieces and, working on a lightly floured surface so the
marzipan doesn't stick, knead a different food coloring into each piece until
evenly colored (see page 6).

Put the butter and sugar in a large bowl and beat with a wooden spoon or an
electric hand beater until pale and creamy. Gradually beat in the eggs a little at
a time, adding a spoonful of the flour if the mixture starts to curdle. Stir in the
almond extract and ground almonds with a large metal spoon. Add the flour and
fold in gently using a large metal spoon until evenly combined. Stir in the milk.

Spoon a thin layer of the mixture into the pan and level the surface. Roll out
one marzipan color on a lightly floured surface until slightly smaller than the
diameter of the pan. Position the marzipan disc on top of the mixture in the
pan and spread with one-quarter of the remaining cake mixture. Repeat rolling
and layering, finishing with a layer of cake mixture. Bake for 1¾ hours or until
risen and firm to the touch and a skewer inserted into the center of the cake
comes out clean. Carefully invert the cake onto a cooling rack and allow to
cool before removing the pan and lining paper.

TO DECORATE

Transfer the cake to a plate. Melt the apricot jelly in a small saucepan with a
teaspoon of water. Press the mixture through a small sieve and brush it over the
top and sides of the cake. Working on a lightly floured surface so the marzipan
doesn't stick, knead lilac food coloring into the marzipan until evenly colored.
Roll out to a 12-inch (30-cm) round on a surface dusted with confectioners'
sugar. Lift over the cake and ease around the sides so there are no folds and
creases. Trim off the excess around the base. Dust the top of the cake with
confectioners' sugar and tie a ribbon around the cake's circumference.

# LEOPARD PRINT CAKE

◇◇◇◇◇◇◇◇◇◇◇◇◇◇◇◇◇◇◇◇◇◇◇◇◇◇◇◇◇◇◇◇◇◇◇◇

2¼ sticks (250 g) slightly salted butter, softened, plus extra for greasing

7 oz (200 g) semisweet chocolate, broken into pieces

Generous 1 cup (225 g) superfine sugar

4 large eggs, beaten

2¼ cups (275 g) self-rising flour

⅔ cup (100 g) cornmeal

2 teaspoons vanilla extract

Yellow food coloring

4 tablespoons whole milk

## TO DECORATE

1 quantity Dark Chocolate Ganache (see page 5)

### TO MAKE THE CAKE

Preheat the oven to 325°F (160°C). Grease and line the base and sides of a 6-inch (15-cm) square cake pan (see page 7). Grease the paper. Melt the chocolate in a large heatproof bowl set over a saucepan of gently simmering water. Stir in ¼ stick (25 g) of the butter, and then allow to cool.

Put the remaining butter and the sugar in a large bowl and beat with a wooden spoon or an electric hand beater until pale and creamy. Gradually beat in the eggs a little at a time, adding a spoonful of the flour if the mixture starts to curdle. Add the flour, three-quarters (75 g) of the cornmeal, and the vanilla extract and fold in gently using a large metal spoon. Spoon 3½ oz (100g) of the mixture into a separate bowl and stir the remaining cornmeal and a little yellow food coloring into this mixture. Spoon the colored mixture into a paper pastry bag or small food bag (see page 6) and snip off the tip so the paste can be piped in a line about ⅓ inch (7–8 mm) wide. Stir the milk into the remaining mixture and spread a very thin layer into the base of the pan.

Using a teaspoon, drizzle three lines of melted chocolate across the pan, spacing them roughly equally apart. Each line of chocolate should be about ½ inch (1 cm) wide but need not be neat or even. Pipe a line of the yellow cake mixture over the chocolate. Spoon a little more chocolate over the yellow lines. At this point make a mark on the pan or lining paper to indicate which way the chocolate lines are piped. Freeze the pan for 10–15 minutes to firm up the chocolate. Carefully spoon a thin layer of uncolored cake mixture over the chocolate then add more chocolate and yellow lines (in the same direction as the first), this time staggering their positioning so they are not directly over the first row. Chill again to lightly set. Repeat the layering of uncolored cake mixture and chocolate and yellow lines, finishing with uncolored cake mixture.

Bake for about 1 hour 20 minutes or until firm to the touch and a skewer inserted into the center comes out clean. Transfer to a cooling rack to cool, keeping a note again of which way the piped lines run for when you cut the cake.

## TO DECORATE

Remove the lining paper and transfer the cake to a serving plate. Using a
spatula, spread the top and sides with an even layer of dark chocolate ganache.

SERVES 12–14
PREPARATION AND DECORATING TIME
ABOUT 1¼ HOURS, PLUS COOLING
AND FREEZING

2⅝ sticks (300 g) slightly
   salted butter, cut into
   pieces, plus extra for
   greasing
2½ cups (300 g) self-rising
   flour, plus extra for
   dusting
1½ cups (300 g) light brown
   sugar
8 oz (250 g) semisweet
   chocolate, chopped
4 large eggs, beaten
2 teaspoons vanilla extract
¼ cup (25 g) unsweetened
   cocoa powder

TO DECORATE
1 quart (1 liter) raspberry
   ripple ice cream
1 quantity Meringue
   Frosting (see page 5)

# RED VELVET RIPPLE CAKE

||||||||||||||||||||||||||||||||||||||||||||||||||||||||||||||

### TO MAKE THE CAKE

Preheat the oven to 350°F (180°C). Grease and base-line 2 × 7-inch (18-cm) round layer pans and dust the sides with flour (see page 7). Put the butter, sugar, and chocolate in a large saucepan and heat gently, stirring frequently, until the chocolate has melted. Avoid letting the mixture boil. Remove from the heat once the ingredients are smoothly combined and set aside to cool for 5 minutes.

Stir in the eggs and vanilla extract. Sift the flour and cocoa powder into the pan and fold in gently using a large metal spoon until combined. Divide half the mixture between the two pans, spreading it to the edges. Bake for 25 minutes until just firm to the touch. Allow to cool in the pans for 10 minutes. Loosen the edges with a knife and carefully invert onto a cooling rack to cool, leaving the lining paper intact. Wash the layer pans and grease and re-line them. Bake the remaining mixture in the same way.

### TO DECORATE

Using a metal ice-cream scoop, carefully scoop out semi-circles of cake from the 4 layers. You should be able to take 6–7 scoops from each cake layer. Use a wiggling action as you cut through the sponge to stop it tearing. (Freeze the scooped out sponge for another time—see page 7.) Take half-scoops of the ice cream and place them in the hollows in the sponge. You might need to let the ice cream soften first. Washing the scoop in hot water frequently will make scooping easier. Stack the ice cream-filled cakes on a freezerproof serving plate and freeze while making the meringue frosting.

Spread the frosting all over the top and sides of the cake with a spatula and return the cake to the freezer for at least 6 hours or overnight before serving.

To serve, transfer the cake to the fridge for about 1 hour before slicing.

# WHITE **CHOCOLATE** CRISPY **CAKE**

4 oz (125 g) semisweet or milk chocolate, broken into pieces

7 oz (200 g) white chocolate, broken into pieces

7 cups (175 g) unsweetened puffed rice cereal

About 1 cup (150 g) colorful mixed dried fruits, such as kiwi, mango, cherries, tangerines, cranberries, and blueberries, roughly chopped if in large pieces

Scant 1 cup (40 g) mini marshmallows, plus extra chopped mini marshmallows to decorate

TO DECORATE
½ quantity White Chocolate Ganache (see page 5)

## TO MAKE THE CAKE

Dampen a 6-inch (15-cm) square cake pan and line with a large square of plastic wrap, pressing it carefully into the corners and up the sides. Melt the semisweet or milk chocolate in a small heatproof bowl set over a saucepan of gently simmering water. Melt the white chocolate in a large heatproof bowl in the same way.

Stir the puffed rice cereal into the bowl of white chocolate. Once combined, add the mixed dried fruits and marshmallows and stir well to mix.

Spoon one-third of the cereal mixture into the pan and spread it into the corners. Use the back of a wetted spoon to press the mixture down gently. Spoon one-half of the melted semisweet or milk chocolate on top, spreading it in a thin layer.

Spoon half the remaining cereal mixture on top, spreading it and packing it down as before. Spread with the remaining melted semisweet or milk chocolate and then the rest of the cereal mixture. Set aside for at least 1 hour to firm up.

## TO DECORATE

Turn the cake out of the pan, peel away the plastic wrap and transfer the cake to a serving plate. Using a spatula, spread the white chocolate ganache over the top and sides of the cake in an even layer. Arrange extra mini marshmallows over the cake to decorate. Store in a cool place, preferably not the fridge, until ready to serve.

SERVES 10–12
PREPARATION AND DECORATING TIME
ABOUT 1 HOUR, PLUS COOLING

2 sticks (225 g) slightly
salted butter, softened,
plus extra for greasing

Generous 1 cup (225 g)
superfine sugar

2 teaspoons vanilla extract

4 large eggs, beaten

2¾ cups (350 g) self-rising
flour

7 oz (200 g) pumpkin or
butternut squash, skinned,
seeded, and finely grated

1½ oz (40 g) fresh ginger
root, peeled and
finely grated (about
1½ tablespoons)

Orange food coloring

3 tablespoons (25 g) poppy
seeds, plus extra to
decorate

4 tablespoons whole milk

TO DECORATE
1 quantity Vanilla
Buttercream (see page 4)

# POPPY SEED AND PUMPKIN MARBLE CAKE

◇◇◇◇◇◇◇◇◇◇◇◇◇◇◇◇◇◇◇◇◇◇◇◇◇◇◇◇◇◇◇◇

### TO MAKE THE CAKE

Preheat the oven to 325°F (160°C). Grease and line the base and sides of
a 6-inch (15-cm) square cake pan (see page 7). Grease the paper.

Put the butter, sugar, and vanilla extract in a large bowl and beat with a wooden
spoon or an electric hand beater until pale and creamy. Gradually beat in the
eggs a little at a time, adding a spoonful of the flour if the mixture starts to
curdle. Add the flour and fold in gently using a large metal spoon. Divide the
mixture between two bowls. Stir the pumpkin or squash and ginger into one
bowl and add a little orange food coloring (see page 6). Stir the poppy seeds
and milk into the other bowl.

Place heaping teaspoonfuls of the pumpkin mixture into the pan, leaving
gaps in between. Fill the spaces with heaping teaspoonfuls of the poppy-seed
mixture. Spoon more mixture on top, alternating the colors so the poppy-
seed mixture is spooned over the pumpkin mixture. Repeat layering until
both mixtures are used up. Run a knife through the two flavors to lightly
marble them together.

Bake for 1 hour 20 minutes or until firm to the touch and a skewer inserted
into the center comes out clean. Transfer to a cooling rack to cool before
removing the lining paper.

### TO DECORATE

Place the cake on a plate and use a spatula to spread the top and sides with
an even layer of vanilla buttercream. Sprinkle lines of poppy seeds over the
top of the cake to decorate.

SERVES 10
PREPARATION AND DECORATING TIME
ABOUT 1 HOUR, PLUS COOLING

Vegetable oil, for greasing

1 cup (125 g) all-purpose
flour, plus extra for
dusting

8 large egg whites

1 teaspoon cream of tartar

1 cup (200 g) superfine
sugar

1 teaspoon rose extract

Pink food coloring

## TO DECORATE

½ quantity Coconut Frosting
(see page 4)

Several fresh pink-edged
white roses

# PINK HEART CAKE

## TO MAKE THE CAKE

Preheat the oven to 325°F (160°C). Grease and base-line a 12 × 7 inch (30 × 18 cm) shallow baking pan or roasting pan of similar dimensions and a 5-cup (1.25-liter) loaf pan (see page 7). Dust with flour so both bases and sides are coated and tap out the excess. Beat the egg whites in a large, spotlessly clean bowl using an electric hand beater until foamy. Add the cream of tartar and continue to beat until the mixture forms soft peaks. Gradually add the sugar, a tablespoonful at a time, beating well after each addition until the mixture is thick and glossy. Add the rose extract with the last of the sugar.

Sift the flour into the bowl and fold in gently using a large metal spoon. Transfer 9¾ oz (275 g) of the mixture to a separate bowl and color deep pink with food coloring (see page 6). Spread the pink mixture into the shallow pan and level the surface. Bake for 12 minutes until just firm to the touch. Turn out onto a parchment paper-lined cooling rack. Allow to cool for 30 minutes.

Spoon half the remaining cake mixture into the loaf pan. Using a 2-inch (5-cm) heart cutter (measured from the dip at the top to the bottom point), cut out as many heart shapes as you can from the pink cake so there is as little waste as possible. Stack the hearts together and arrange the pointed tips uppermost along the length of the pan. You should have enough to pack the hearts tightly into the pan. Press the hearts down gently into the cake mixture so that the tips are lower than the top of the pan. Add the remaining cake mixture to the pan and level the surface. Bake for 20 minutes or until just firm to the touch and a skewer pressed into the white cake comes out clean. Loosen the edges of the cake with a knife. Carefully invert the cake onto a parchment paper-lined cooling rack and allow to cool before removing the pan and lining paper.

## TO DECORATE

Place the cake on a plate and use a spatula to spread the coconut frosting over the top and sides in an even layer. Arrange a row of pink-edged white roses along the top of the cake to serve.

2⅝ sticks (300 g) slightly
salted butter, plus extra
for greasing

2½ cups (300 g) self-rising
flour, plus extra for
dusting

1½ cups (300 g) superfine
sugar

Finely grated zest of
2 small oranges, plus
3 tablespoons juice

5 large eggs

Red, yellow, orange, and
black food coloring

## TO DECORATE

1 quantity Cream Cheese
Frosting (see page 4)

multicolored sugar
sprinkles, to scatter

# FUNKY **PATTERN CAKE**

◇◇◇◇◇◇◇◇◇◇◇◇◇◇◇◇◇◇◇◇◇◇◇◇◇◇◇◇

## TO MAKE THE CAKE

Preheat the oven to 350°F (180°C). Grease and base-line 2 × 8-inch (20-cm)
round layer pans and dust the sides with flour (see page 7). Put the butter,
sugar, orange zest and juice, flour, and eggs in a large bowl and beat with an
electric hand beater until the mixture is pale and creamy. Divide the mixture
evenly between 4 bowls. Add red food coloring to one bowl, yellow to the
second, orange to the third, and black to the last. Work the coloring into each
bowl of cake mixture (see page 6).

Make 4 large paper pastry bags (see page 6) and spoon a colored mixture
into each bag. Snip off the tips so that the mixtures can be piped in lines about
¾ inch (2 cm) thick. Pipe a circle of red mixture around the edge of one pan,
then a circle of black inside it. Continue to pipe, alternating the colors until
you reach the center of the pan. Use the same technique in the other pan. Add
a second layer of circles in the pans, this time using the yellow and orange
mixtures. Repeat until all the cake mixture is used up.

Bake for 30–35 minutes or until just firm to the touch. Loosen the edges of
the cakes with a knife and transfer to a cooling rack to cool before removing
the lining paper.

## TO DECORATE

Use about one-third of the cream cheese frosting to sandwich the cakes
together on a serving plate. Using a spatula, spread a thin layer of frosting
around the sides of the cake to seal in the crumbs. Spread the remaining
frosting over the top and sides of the cake in an even layer and decorate
with multicolored sugar sprinkles.

# SPRINKLE SPECKLED CAKE

• • • • • • • • • • • • • • • • • • • • • • • • • • • • • • • • • • • • •

1½ sticks (175 g) slightly salted butter, softened, plus extra for greasing

Scant 1½ cups (175 g) self-rising flour, plus extra for dusting

Generous ¾ cup (175 g) superfine sugar

3 large eggs

1 teaspoon baking powder

1 tablespoon whole milk

½ cup (100 g) multicolored sugar sprinkles, plus extra to decorate

TO DECORATE

¾ cup (75 g) fresh or defrosted frozen raspberries, plus extra for topping

1¼ sticks (150 g) unsalted butter, softened

1¾ cups (250 g) confectioners' sugar

## TO MAKE THE CAKE

Preheat the oven to 350°F (180°C). Grease and base-line 2 × 7-inch (18-cm) round layer pans and dust the sides with flour (see page 7). Put the butter, sugar, eggs, flour, and baking powder in a large bowl and beat with an electric hand beater until the mixture is pale and creamy. Stir in the milk.

Stir the sugar sprinkles into the cake mixture, divide the mixture between the two layer pans and bake for 25 minutes or until just firm to the touch. Loosen the edges of the cakes with a knife and transfer to a cooling rack to cool before removing the lining paper.

## TO DECORATE

Press the raspberries through a sieve to extract as much juice as possible. Put the raspberry pulp in a large bowl with the butter and confectioners' sugar and beat with a wooden spoon or an electric hand beater until smooth and creamy.

Using a spatula, sandwich the cakes together on a plate with a little of the buttercream. Spread a thin layer of buttercream around the sides of the cake to seal in the crumbs. Spread the remaining buttercream over the top and sides in an even layer.

Arrange a pile of raspberries on the center of the cake and serve scattered with extra sugar sprinkles.

Vegetable oil, for greasing

1 cup (125 g) all-purpose
flour, plus extra for
dusting

8 large egg whites

1 teaspoon cream of tartar

1 cup (200 g) superfine
sugar

2 teaspoons vanilla extract

Turquoise liquid food
coloring (or mix blue
coloring with a little green
to make a turquoise color)

TO DECORATE
1 quantity Coconut Frosting
(see page 4)

# DIP DYE CAKE

## TO MAKE THE CAKE

Preheat the oven to 350°F (180°C). Grease and base-line 2 × 6-inch (15-cm)
round layer pans and dust the sides with flour (see page 7). Beat the egg whites
in a large, spotlessly clean bowl using an electric hand beater until foamy. Add
the cream of tartar and continue to beat until the mixture forms soft peaks.
Gradually add the sugar, a tablespoonful at a time, beating well after each
addition until the mixture is thick and glossy. Add the vanilla extract with the
last of the sugar.

Sift the flour into the bowl and fold in gently using a large metal spoon.
Weigh the mixture and divide the weight by six. Spoon one-sixth of the mixture
(approximately 3½ oz/100 g) into one of the pans and divide the remaining
mixture evenly among 5 bowls. (Small bowls such as cereal bowls are ideal.)
Add a drop of food coloring to the first bowl, a little more to the second, and
so on, until the final bowl is a deep shade of turquoise. Check that there is
a noticeable difference between the color shades, if necessary adding more
coloring to one or two bowls. Spoon the palest color into the second pan and
level the surfaces.

Bake for 12 minutes or until just firm to the touch. Loosen the edges of the
cakes with a knife and turn out onto a parchment paper-lined cooling rack.
Allow to cool with the lining paper intact. Wash the layer pans and grease
and re-line them. Bake the remaining mixtures in the same way. Turn each
of the cakes out to cool then peel away the lining paper.

## TO DECORATE

Place the darkest cake layer on a plate and use a spatula to spread with
4 tablespoons of the frosting. Place the next cake layer on top and spread
with another 4 tablespoons of the coconut frosting. Continue to layer up the
cakes with frosting, finishing with the uncolored cake at the top. Spread
the remaining frosting over the top and sides of the cake.

# CHOCOLATE, RED VELVET, AND VANILLA CAKE

**FOR THE CHOCOLATE CAKE**

1⅛ sticks (125 g) slightly salted butter, softened, plus extra for greasing

Generous ½ cup (125 g) superfine sugar

2 large eggs

¾ cup (100 g) self-rising flour

½ teaspoon baking powder

¼ cup (25 g) unsweetened cocoa powder

**FOR THE RED VELVET CAKE**

Scant 1½ cups (175 g) all-purpose flour

1 teaspoon baking soda

1 cup (200 g) superfine sugar

½ cup (75 g) finely grated beet (about ½ small beet)

1¼ sticks (150 g) slightly salted butter, melted

3 large eggs

3 tablespoons whole milk

Red food coloring

**FOR THE VANILLA CAKE**

1⅛ sticks (125 g) slightly salted butter, softened

Generous ½ cup (125 g) superfine sugar

2 large eggs

1 cup (125 g) self-rising flour

½ teaspoon baking powder

1 teaspoon vanilla extract

**TO DECORATE**

1 quantity Dark Chocolate Ganache (see page 5)

## TO MAKE THE CHOCOLATE CAKE

Preheat the oven to 350°F (180°C). Grease and line the base and sides of a 7-inch (18-cm) square cake pan. Grease the paper. Put all the ingredients in a large bowl and beat well with an electric hand beater until smooth and creamy. Turn the mixture into the pan and level the surface. Bake for 30 minutes or until just firm to the touch. Loosen the edges with a knife and transfer to a cooling rack to cool before removing the lining paper. Keep the oven on.

## TO MAKE THE RED VELVET CAKE

Grease and line the pan as above. Combine the flour, baking soda, and sugar in a large bowl. Stir in the grated beet. Mix together the butter, eggs, and milk in a separate bowl and add to the cake mixture. Stir well to combine and add a little red food coloring (see page 6). Turn the mixture into the pan and bake as above, allowing 35–40 minutes or until just firm to the touch. Loosen the edges with a knife and transfer to a cooling rack to cool. Keep the oven on.

## TO MAKE THE VANILLA CAKE

Grease and line the pan as above. Put all the ingredients in a bowl and beat well with an electric hand beater until smooth and creamy. Turn the mixture into the pan and level the surface. Bake as above for 30 minutes or until just firm to the touch. Loosen the edges with a knife and transfer to a cooling rack to cool.

## TO DECORATE

Place the cakes side by side on the work surface and slice off the tops so they are all exactly the same height. Trim a ½-inch (1-cm) slice off the sides of all the cakes. (Freeze all the trimmings for another time—see page 7.)

Stack the cakes together and cut them in half vertically. Put one stack to one side and slice the remaining stack in half vertically. Put half to one side again and cut the remaining stack in half vertically once more. Rearrange all the cake

pieces together in a block to create a cake of three layers in contrasting flavors and sizes.

Separate the layers and place the first on a serving plate. Using a spatula, secure the pieces together with a little dark chocolate ganache. Spread the top with a thin layer of ganache. Arrange the second layer of cakes on top, securing them with more ganache and spreading another layer on top. Add the final layer of cake, securing it in the same way. Spread a thin layer of ganache over the top and sides of the cake to seal in the crumbs. Spread the remaining ganache over the cake, drawing the edge of the spatula across it to give a textured surface.

SERVES 12–14
PREPARATION AND DECORATING TIME
ABOUT 1¾–2 HOURS, PLUS
OVERNIGHT COOLING

# CHRISTMAS SNOW CAKE

||||||||||||||||||||||||||||||||||||||||||||||||||||||||||||||||||||||||||||

## FOR THE FIRST CAKE

1½ sticks (175 g) slightly
   salted butter, softened,
   plus extra for greasing

Generous ¾ cup (175 g)
   superfine sugar

3 large eggs

Scant 1⅔ cups (200 g)
   self-rising flour

Bright green food coloring

## FOR THE SECOND CAKE

2¼ cups (275 g) self-rising
   flour, plus extra for
   dusting

2 sticks (225 g) slightly
   salted butter, softened

Generous 1 cup (225 g)
   superfine sugar

3 large eggs, beaten

1 teaspoon almond extract

1 cup (100 g) ground
   almonds

3 tablespoons whole milk

1 teaspoon baking powder

Blue food coloring

## TO DECORATE

4 tablespoons apricot jelly

1 lb 12 oz (800 g) marzipan

Confectioners' sugar, for
   dusting

2 lb (1 kg) white ready-
   to-use icing

Snowflake sprinkles,
   to decorate

### TO MAKE THE FIRST CAKE

Preheat the oven to 325°F (160°C). Grease and line the bases and sides of a 7-inch (18-cm) round cake pan and a 10¼ × 7 inch (26 × 18 cm) shallow baking pan (see page 7). Grease and base-line a ½-cup (125-ml) dariole mold. Grease the paper. Put all the ingredients for the first cake except the food coloring in a large bowl and beat with an electric hand beater until smooth and creamy. Spoon 9 oz (250 g) of the mixture into the round pan. Beat a little bright green food coloring into the remainder of the mixture (see page 6). Spoon about 2¾ oz (75 g) of the colored mixture into the dariole mold then turn the remainder into the shallow pan and level the surfaces of all the cakes. Bake the cakes for 25 minutes or until risen and just firm to the touch. Leave the round cake in the pan and transfer the other cakes to a cooling rack to cool. Keep the oven on.

### TO MAKE THE SECOND CAKE

Beat together all the ingredients except the food coloring with an electric hand beater until pale and creamy. Spoon 5¼ oz (150 g) of the mixture into a paper pastry bag or plastic food bag (see page 6). Stir blue food coloring into the remaining mixture until colored deep blue (see page 6). Put in a large paper pastry bag or plastic food bag.

Using a 2½-inch (6-cm) Christmas-tree cutter, cut out tree shapes from the green-colored cake in the shallow baking pan. Arrange the shapes in a circle on top of the cake in the round pan, with the trees standing upright. Pack the trees tightly together, side by side, and keep the outer edges of the trees at least ¾ inch (1.5 cm) away from the sides of the pan. Cut a cone shape from the small cake to represent a Christmas-tree shape and place this in the center of the pan. Snip off a ½-inch (1-cm) tip from the end of the blue cake mixture bag and pipe a layer over the cake base. Snip off a smaller tip from the bag of uncolored cake mixture so the mixture flows out in a ¼-inch (5-mm) thick line. Pipe several circles of cake mixture over the blue mixture. Pipe a further layer of blue, then more white circles. Continue layering up the colors until

all the mixtures have been used. Bake for 1 hour 40 minutes or until firm to the touch and a skewer inserted into the center of the blue cake comes out clean. Transfer to a wire rack to cool.

### TO DECORATE

Transfer the cake to a plate. Melt the apricot jelly in a small saucepan with a teaspoon of water. Press the mixture through a sieve and brush it over the top and sides of the cake. Roll out the marzipan on a surface dusted with confectioners' sugar until you have a circle measuring 13 inches (33 cm) in diameter. Lift the marzipan over the cake and ease

it down the sides so it fits without any creases. Trim off the excess around the base of the cake.

Knead a little blue food coloring into 1 lb 8 oz (700 g) of the white ready-to-use icing (see page 6). Roll it out on a surface dusted with confectioners' sugar until you have a circle measuring 13 inches (33 cm) in diameter and use it to cover the cake using the same method as for the marzipan. Thinly roll out the remaining white ready-to-use icing until about 9 inches (23 cm) in diameter. Cut a wavy edge around the circle and lift the icing over the cake. Smooth out so the icing falls down the sides of the cake. Scatter with snowflake sprinkles.

# POLKA DOT CAKE

● ● ● ● ● ● ● ● ● ● ● ● ● ● ● ● ● ● ● ● ● ● ● ● ●

2⅝ sticks (300 g) slightly
   salted butter, softened,
   plus extra for greasing

2½ cups (300 g) self-rising
   flour, plus extra for
   dusting

1½ cups (300 g) superfine
   sugar

Finely grated zest
   of 3 lemons, plus
   3 tablespoons juice

5 large eggs

Pink and yellow food
   coloring

## TO DECORATE

1 quantity Lemon
   Buttercream (see page 4)

2 oz (50 g) pink ready-
   to-use icing

Confectioners' sugar,
   for dusting

## TO MAKE THE CAKE

Preheat the oven to 350°F (180°C). Grease and base-line 3 × 7-inch (18-cm) round layer pans and dust the sides with flour (see page 7). Put the butter, sugar, and lemon zest in a large bowl and beat with a wooden spoon or an electric hand beater until pale and creamy. Gradually beat in the eggs a little at a time, adding a spoonful of the flour if the mixture starts to curdle. Stir in the lemon juice, then add the flour and fold in gently using a large metal spoon until just combined.

Transfer 5¼ oz (150 g) of the mixture to another bowl and stir in a little pink food coloring (see page 6). Transfer the mixture to a paper pastry bag (see page 6) and snip off the tip so the mixture flows out in a ¼-inch (5-mm) thick line when gently squeezed.

Add a little yellow food coloring into the remaining mixture and spread a ¼-inch (5-mm) depth of the yellow mixture into the pans. Pipe circles of the pink mixture over the top, gradually working in toward the center and keeping the circles about ¾ inch (1.5 cm) apart. Transfer the remaining yellow mixture to another paper pastry bag and snip off the tip so the mixture flows out in a thicker line than the pink mixture. Pipe thicker circles of the yellow mixture between the pink. Pipe more circles of pink on top making sure the circles are over the yellow cake mixture. Fill in with more circles of yellow mixture. Continue piping until the mixtures are used up.

Bake for 25 minutes or until just firm to the touch. Loosen the edges of the cakes with a knife and transfer to a cooling rack to cool before removing the lining paper.

## TO DECORATE

Using a spatula, sandwich the cake layers together on a plate using one-third of the lemon buttercream. Spoon 2 tablespoons buttercream into a small pastry bag. Spread the remainder of the buttercream over the top and sides of the cake in an even layer.

To make the flowers, thinly roll out the pink icing on a surface dusted with confectioners' sugar. Cut out small flower shapes using a ¾-inch (1.5-cm) cutter and arrange around the base of the cake. Cut off the merest tip from the pastry bag containing the buttercream and pipe a dot into the center of each flower.

# **BLACK** AND **WHITE** CAKE

7 large egg whites

1 teaspoon cream of tartar

Generous ¾ cup (175 g)
superfine sugar

2 teaspoons vanilla extract

¾ cup (100 g) all-purpose
flour

Black paste food coloring

## TO DECORATE

5 tablespoons (75 g)
unsalted butter, softened,
plus extra for greasing

¾ cup (125 g) confectioners'
sugar, plus extra for
dusting

1 lb 12 oz (800 g) white
ready-to-use icing

2 oz (50 g) black ready-to-
use icing

4 ft (1.2 m) black and white
polka-dot ribbon, about
1 inch (2.5 cm) wide

## TO MAKE THE CAKE

Preheat the oven to 325°F (160°C). Grease the base and side of a 7-inch
(18-cm) round cake pan and the outside of an empty 14-oz (400-g) food can
(see page 7) and position the food can in the center of the pan, opened end
face-up, to shape a ring pan. Line the base and side of the pan and the outside
of the can. Grease the paper. Beat the egg whites in a large, spotlessly clean
bowl using an electric hand beater until foamy. Add the cream of tartar and
continue to beat until the mixture forms soft peaks. Gradually add the sugar,
a tablespoonful at a time, beating well after each addition until the mixture
is thick and glossy. Add the vanilla extract with the last of the sugar.

Sift the flour into the bowl and fold in gently using a large metal spoon.
Transfer 5¼ oz (150 g) of the mixture to another bowl and color dark gray
using the black food coloring (see page 6). Spread a little of the white cake
mixture into the base of the pan and spread a little gray mixture on top. Repeat
layering, finishing with a layer of white cake mixture. (The layers need not be
evenly spread and will look effective if irregular.) Fill the food can with pie
weights (or dried beans or lentils that you use for baking blind).

Bake for 25 minutes or until just firm to the touch and a skewer, pierced
through the center of the cake, comes out clean. Allow to cool in the pan.

## TO DECORATE

Beat together the butter and confectioners' sugar with a wooden spoon or
electric hand beater until smooth and creamy. Add 1 teaspoon hot water and
beat again until very pale. Remove the food can from the center of the cake
and turn the cake out of the pan by inverting onto a serving plate. Remove the
lining paper and use a spatula to spread the buttercream over the top and sides
of the cake.

Roll out 5¼ oz (150 g) of the white ready-to-use icing on a surface dusted with
confectioners' sugar and trim to a strip whose width is the same as the depth

of the cake and whose length is 8 inches (20 cm). Use to line the hole in the center of the cake, smoothing the icing as neatly as possible. Roll out the remaining icing to an 11-inch (28-cm) round. Cut out a 2¼-inch (5.5-cm) circle from the center and lift the icing over the cake so the cut-out circle is in line with the hole in the center of the cake. Ease the icing around the sides of the cake to fit, trimming off the excess around the base.

Thinly roll out the black ready-to-use icing and cut out small circles using ½ and ¾ inch (1 and 2 cm) round cutters. Secure the circles on the top of the cake with a dampened paintbrush and tie a ribbon around the cake's circumference.

SERVES 12
PREPARATION AND DECORATING TIME
ABOUT 1 HOUR, PLUS OVERNIGHT
COOLING AND CHILLING

1⅛ sticks (125 g) slightly
 salted butter, softened,
 plus extra for greasing

Generous ½ cup (125 g)
 superfine sugar

Finely grated zest of 2 limes,
 plus 2 tablespoons juice

2 large eggs, beaten

1¼ cups (150 g) self-rising
 flour

Lime green food coloring

TO DECORATE

1 lb 2 oz (600 g) soft fruit
 jellies

2 cups (450 g) cream cheese

5 tablespoons superfine
 sugar

1 tablespoon unflavored
 gelatin powder

Scant ½ cup (100 ml)
 whole milk

2 limes

1¼ cups (300 ml) heavy
 cream

2 tablespoons confectioners'
 sugar

# JELLY JEWEL CAKE

◇◇◇◇◇◇◇◇◇◇◇◇◇◇◇◇◇◇◇◇◇◇◇◇◇◇◇◇◇◇◇◇

TO MAKE THE CAKE

Preheat the oven to 325°F (160°C). Grease and line the base and side of a
7-inch (18-cm) round cake pan (see page 7). Grease the paper. Put the butter,
sugar, and lime zest in a large bowl and beat with a wooden spoon or an
electric hand beater until pale and creamy. Gradually beat in the eggs a little
at a time, adding a spoonful of the flour if the mixture starts to curdle. Add the
flour and fold in gently using a large metal spoon until evenly combined. Stir
in the lime juice and a little lime green food coloring (see page 6).

Turn the mixture into the pan and level the surface. Bake for about 45 minutes
or until firm to the touch and a skewer inserted into the center comes out
clean. Transfer to a cooling rack and allow to cool, preferably overnight, before
removing the lining paper.

TO DECORATE

Cut the cake horizontally into 3 layers. Cut each fruit jelly into about 4 pieces
so each piece is roughly ¾ inch (1.5 cm) in diameter. Beat the cream cheese
with 3 tablespoons of the sugar in a large bowl with a wooden spoon to soften.
Sprinkle the gelatin powder over 2 tablespoons cold water in a small bowl and
set aside for 5 minutes. Bring the milk to a boil in a small saucepan. Remove
from the heat and stir in the gelatin until dissolved. Beat the milk into the
cream cheese mixture and stir in the chopped jellies.

Place one cake layer on a serving plate and tip half the cream cheese mixture
onto it. Spread to the edges in an even layer and position another cake layer
on top. Spread the remaining cream cheese mixture on top and position the
remaining cake layer.

Pare the zest from the limes and mix with the remaining superfine sugar.

Whip the cream with the confectioners' sugar until the mixture forms soft peaks.
Use a spatula to spread a thin layer of the cream over the top and sides of the

cake to seal in the crumbs. Spread the remaining cream over the cake in an even layer. Chill in the refrigerator for at least 6 hours or overnight before serving.

Scatter the lime sugar over the surface just before serving. The jellies inside the cake will start to soften after about 24 hours but will still taste good.

# DOUBLE CHOCOLATE AND BANANA CAKE

**FOR THE BANANA AND WHITE
CHOCOLATE CAKES**

5 tablespoons (75 g) slightly
 salted butter, softened,
 plus extra for greasing

Generous ¼ cup (65 g)
 superfine sugar

1 large egg

3 tablespoons whole milk

1 cup (125 g) self-rising
 flour

½ teaspoon baking powder

1 small ripe banana, mashed

2 oz (50 g) white chocolate,
 chopped

Pink food coloring

**FOR THE DARK CHOCOLATE CAKE**

7 oz (200 g) semisweet
 chocolate, chopped

Scant ½ cup (100 ml)
 whole milk

1½ sticks (175 g) slightly
 salted butter, softened

1 cup (200 g) light brown
 sugar

4 large eggs, beaten

1¾ cups (225 g) self-rising
 flour

1 teaspoon baking powder

**TO DECORATE**

1 quantity Vanilla
 Buttercream (see page 4)

### TO MAKE THE BANANA AND WHITE CHOCOLATE CAKES

Preheat the oven to 325°F (160°C). Cover a piece of cardboard that is the same length and depth as a 6-inch (15-cm) square cake pan with aluminum foil and fit it down the center of the pan. Line the bases and sides of the two sections of the pan (see page 7). Grease the paper.

Put the butter, sugar, egg, milk, flour, and baking powder in a large bowl and beat with an electric hand beater until smooth and creamy. Divide the mixture between two bowls. Beat the mashed banana into the mixture in one bowl and the chocolate and food coloring into the mixture in the other (see page 6). Spoon the mixtures into the separate sides of the pan and level the surfaces. Bake for 30–35 minutes until the cakes are risen and firm to the touch. Transfer to a cooling rack to cool before removing the lining paper. Keep the oven on.

### TO MAKE THE DARK CHOCOLATE CAKE

Grease and line the base and side of a 8-inch (20-cm) round cake pan. Grease the paper. Put the chocolate and milk in a small heatproof bowl and melt, either set over a saucepan of gently simmering water or in short spurts in the microwave. Beat the butter and sugar together in a large bowl with a wooden spoon or an electric hand beater until smooth and creamy. Stir in the melted chocolate mixture and the eggs. Add the flour and baking powder and fold in gently using a large metal spoon until mixed. Spread a thin layer into the base of the pan.

Cut the banana and pink chocolate cakes into small, irregularly sized pieces. Some can be small cubes or diced, others stick shapes or thin slices. Scatter a few pieces over the cake mixture in the pan. Spoon more cake mixture on top and scatter with more banana and pink chocolate cake shapes. Continue to layer, finishing with cake mixture. Bake for about 1¼ hours or until firm to the touch and a skewer inserted into the center of the dark chocolate cake comes out clean. Allow to cool in the pan for 15 minutes before transferring to a cooling rack to cool completely and removing the lining paper.

## TO DECORATE

Place the cake on a plate and use a spatula to spread the top and sides with an even layer of vanilla buttercream.

# CHERRY **CUPCAKE** CAKE

◇◇◇◇◇◇◇◇◇◇◇◇◇◇◇◇◇◇◇◇◇◇◇◇◇◇◇◇

## FOR THE FIRST CAKE

1¼ sticks (150 g) slightly salted butter, softened, plus extra for greasing

¾ cup (150 g) superfine sugar

3 large eggs

1¼ cups (150 g) self-rising flour

¼ cup (25 g) ground almonds

Pink food coloring, plus extra to decorate

## FOR THE SECOND CAKE

1¾ sticks (200 g) slightly salted butter, softened

1 cup (200 g) superfine sugar

3 large eggs

Scant 1⅔ cups (200 g) self-rising flour

1 cup (100 g) ground almonds

1½ teaspoons almond extract

3 tablespoons whole milk

8–10 graham crackers

¾ cup (150 g) natural candied cherries

## TO DECORATE

½ quantity Vanilla Buttercream (see page 4)

2 tablespoons superfine sugar

## TO MAKE THE FIRST CAKE

Preheat the oven to 325°F (160°C). Cover a piece of cardboard that is the same length and depth as an 8-inch (20-cm) square cake pan with aluminum foil and fit it into the pan 2½ inches (6 cm) in from one side. Line the large rectangular section with wax paper (see page 7). Grease the paper.

Put all the ingredients for the first cake, except the food coloring, in a large bowl and beat with an electric hand beater until pale and creamy. Add a little pink food coloring (see page 6). Turn the mixture into the lined section of the pan and level the surface.

Bake for 50 minutes or until just firm to the touch. Transfer to a cooling rack to cool. Wash, grease, and re-line the pan, this time without the cardboard divider.

Cut the cake lengthwise into two pieces so that one piece is twice the width of the other. Cut a thin slice off the top of the larger piece of cake to level it then cut the long sides off at a sloping angle to create a simple cupcake shape when viewed at one end. Do the same with the smaller piece of cake, first cutting the top off so it is 1 inch (2.5 cm) deep before cutting the sloping sides. Freeze the cake trimmings for another time (see page 7). Keep the oven on.

## TO MAKE THE SECOND CAKE

Put the butter, sugar, eggs, flour, ground almonds, and almond extract in a large bowl and beat with an electric hand beater until pale and creamy. Stir in the milk. Spoon 7 oz (200 g) of the mixture into the pan and spread level. Place the two pink cakes on top of the mixture, leaving a space between them. Cut rectangles from the crackers so they are slightly narrower than the widths of the pink cakes. (If the crackers are brittle and break as you cut them, pop each one in the microwave for about 10 seconds to soften them and try again.) Arrange along the tops of the pink cakes. Arrange the cherries down the centers so there are no gaps in between them. Carefully spread a thin layer of cake mixture over the cherries then dot the remainder in between and over the

pink cakes. (The cake mixture will rise up during baking to cover the pink cakes entirely.) Bake for about 1 hour or until a skewer inserted into the white cake comes out clean. Transfer to a cooling rack to cool before removing the lining paper.

TO DECORATE

Place the cake on a serving plate and use a spatula to spread the top and sides with a thin layer of

vanilla buttercream to seal in the crumbs. Put the remaining buttercream in a pastry bag fitted with a star tip (see page 6) and pipe swirls of buttercream all over the top of the cake.

Put the superfine sugar in a small bowl and add a dash of pink food coloring. Use the back of a teaspoon to work the color into the sugar. Sprinkle the colored sugar onto the center of each buttercream swirl to serve.

# CHOCOLATE, FRUIT, AND NUT CAKE

14 oz (400 g) milk chocolate,
broken into pieces

7 tablespoons (100 g)
slightly salted butter,
cut into pieces

3 tablespoons whole milk

2 tablespoons light corn
syrup

3½ oz (100 g) semisweet
chocolate, cut into ½-inch
(1-cm) dice

3½ oz (100 g) soft fudge, cut
into ½-inch (1-cm) dice

Generous ½ cup (100 g)
dried apricots, cut into
½-inch (1-cm) dice

⅔ cup (100 g) whole,
shelled hazelnuts

12 original Oreo cookies

## TO DECORATE

½ quantity Dark Chocolate
Ganache (see page 5)

Milk or semisweet chocolate
curls, to sprinkle

## TO MAKE THE CAKE

Cover a piece of cardboard that is the same length and depth as a 7-inch (18-cm) square cake pan with aluminum foil and fit it down the center of the pan. Line the base and sides of one section of the tin with a large square of plastic wrap, pushing it down into the corners and creasing it up the sides.

Put the milk chocolate in a large heatproof bowl. Add the butter, milk, and syrup. Place over a saucepan of gently simmering water until the chocolate has melted, giving the mixture an occasional, gentle stir. Remove from the heat and allow to cool until completely cold but not beginning to set.

Add the semisweet chocolate, fudge, and apricots to the melted chocolate mixture with the hazelnuts. Stir lightly to mix. Spoon a little into the pan to cover the base. Place a few cookies on top, pressing them down into the chocolate mixture to eliminate any pockets of air. Spoon another thin layer of the chocolate mixture on top and then more cookies. Continue layering, finishing with a thin layer of chocolate. Cover and chill in the refrigerator for several hours until firm.

## TO DECORATE

Lift the chocolate cake out of the pan, peel away the plastic wrap and transfer the cake to a plate. Using a spatula, spread the dark chocolate ganache over the top and sides of the cake in an even layer. Scatter the top with the chocolate curls and refrigerate or keep in a cool place. Serve cut into thin slices.

1½ sticks (175 g) slightly
  salted butter, softened,
  plus extra for greasing

Generous ¾ cup (175 g)
  superfine sugar

2 teaspoons vanilla bean
  paste or extract

3 large eggs, beaten

1¾ cups (225 g) self-rising
  flour

TO DECORATE

2 teaspoons unflavored
  gelatin powder

Scant 1 cup (200 g) cream
  cheese

⅓ cup (75 g) superfine sugar

1¼ cups (300 ml) heavy
  cream

2⅓ cups (350 g) small fresh
  strawberries, plus extra
  to scatter

5 tablespoons freeze-dried
  strawberry pieces

# STRAWBERRY CHEESE CAKE

## TO MAKE THE CAKE

Preheat the oven to 325°F (160°C). Grease and line the base and side of a
7-inch (18-cm) round cake pan (see page 7). Grease the paper. Put the butter,
sugar, and vanilla bean paste or extract in a large bowl and beat with a wooden
spoon or an electric hand beater until pale and creamy. Gradually beat in the
eggs, a little at a time, adding a spoonful of the flour if the mixture starts to
curdle. Add the flour and fold in gently using a large metal spoon until just
combined. Turn the mixture into the pan and level the surface.

Bake for 1–1¼ hours or until firm to the touch and a skewer inserted into the
center of the cake comes out clean. Transfer to a cooling rack to cool before
removing the lining paper.

## TO DECORATE

Using a sharp knife, cut a ½-inch (1-cm) thick slice off the base of the cake
and place this on a serving plate. Cut a ¼-inch (5-mm) thick slice off the top
of the cake and reserve it for a lid. Using a sharp knife cut out the middle of
the center part of the cake, keeping the knife completely vertical and ½ inch
(1 cm) away from the edges of the cake. Carefully lift out the center to leave a
thin shell. (Freeze the center for another time, see page 7.) Position the shell
over the cake base.

Sprinkle the gelatin powder over 2 tablespoons cold water in a small bowl and
set aside for 5 minutes. Beat the cream cheese with the sugar in a bowl with a
wooden spoon or an electric hand beater until softened. Put ⅔ cup (150 ml) of
the cream in a small saucepan and bring just to a boil. Remove from the heat
and stir in the gelatin until dissolved. Pour over the cream cheese mixture and
beat well to mix. Stir in the fresh and dried strawberries.

Turn the mixture into the cake shell and spread gently, taking care so the cake
shell doesn't split. Position the cake lid on top. Whip the remaining cream until
only just holding its shape. Put in a large pastry bag fitted with a large star tip

and pipe vertical lines onto the sides of the cake. Use up the cream by piping it over the top of the cake and use a spatula to spread it in an even layer. Chill for at least 3 hours or overnight. Serve scattered with small strawberries.

# CARROT AND COCONUT BATTENBURG

## FOR THE CARROT CAKE

7 tablespoons (100 g)
slightly salted butter,
softened, plus extra
for greasing

½ cup (100 g) light brown
sugar

2 large eggs

¾ cup (100 g) self-rising
flour

½ teaspoon baking powder

1 teaspoon apple pie spice

¾ cup (75 g) carrots,
finely grated

¼ cup (40 g) dried apricots,
finely chopped

¼ cup (25 g) ground
almonds

Orange food coloring

## FOR THE COCONUT CAKE

7 tablespoons (100 g)
slightly salted butter,
softened

½ cup (100 g) superfine
sugar

2 large eggs

¾ cup (100 g) self-rising
flour

¼ cup (25 g) shredded,
dried coconut

½ teaspoon baking powder

## TO DECORATE

⅔ cup (200 g) apricot jelly

1 lb (475 g) marzipan

Superfine sugar, for dusting

### TO MAKE THE CAKE

Preheat the oven to 350°F (180°C). Cover a piece of cardboard that is the same length and depth as a 8-inch (20-cm) square cake pan with aluminum foil and fit it down the center of the pan. Grease and line the bases and sides of the two sections. Grease the paper.

Put all the ingredients for the carrot cake, except the food coloring, in a large bowl and beat with an electric hand beater until smooth and creamy. Add a little orange food coloring (see page 6). Turn the mixture into one pan section and level the surface.

Put all the ingredients for the coconut cake in a large bowl and beat with an electric hand beater until smooth and creamy. Turn the mixture into the other side of the pan and level the surface. Bake for 40 minutes or until just firm to the touch. Transfer to a cooling rack to cool before removing the lining paper.

### TO DECORATE

Warm the jelly to soften it and press it through a sieve to remove any lumps. Place the cakes side by side on the work surface and use a sharp knife to slice off the tops so they are both exactly the same height. Take a very thin slice off each side of both cakes to remove the crusty edges. Cut each cake lengthwise into 3 even-sized pieces. Stack the pieces of cake together in a checkered pattern, securing them in place with half the jelly.

Sprinkle a dusting of superfine sugar onto a sheet of wax paper. Roll out 13¼ oz (375 g) of the marzipan on the paper and trim to a neat rectangle that is the length of the cake and long enough to wrap around the long sides of the cake. Brush the marzipan thinly with jelly. Place the cake in the center and wrap the marzipan around it. Turn the cake over so the join is underneath. Brush the ends of the cake with the remaining jelly. Roll out the remaining marzipan into two squares and use to cover the ends.

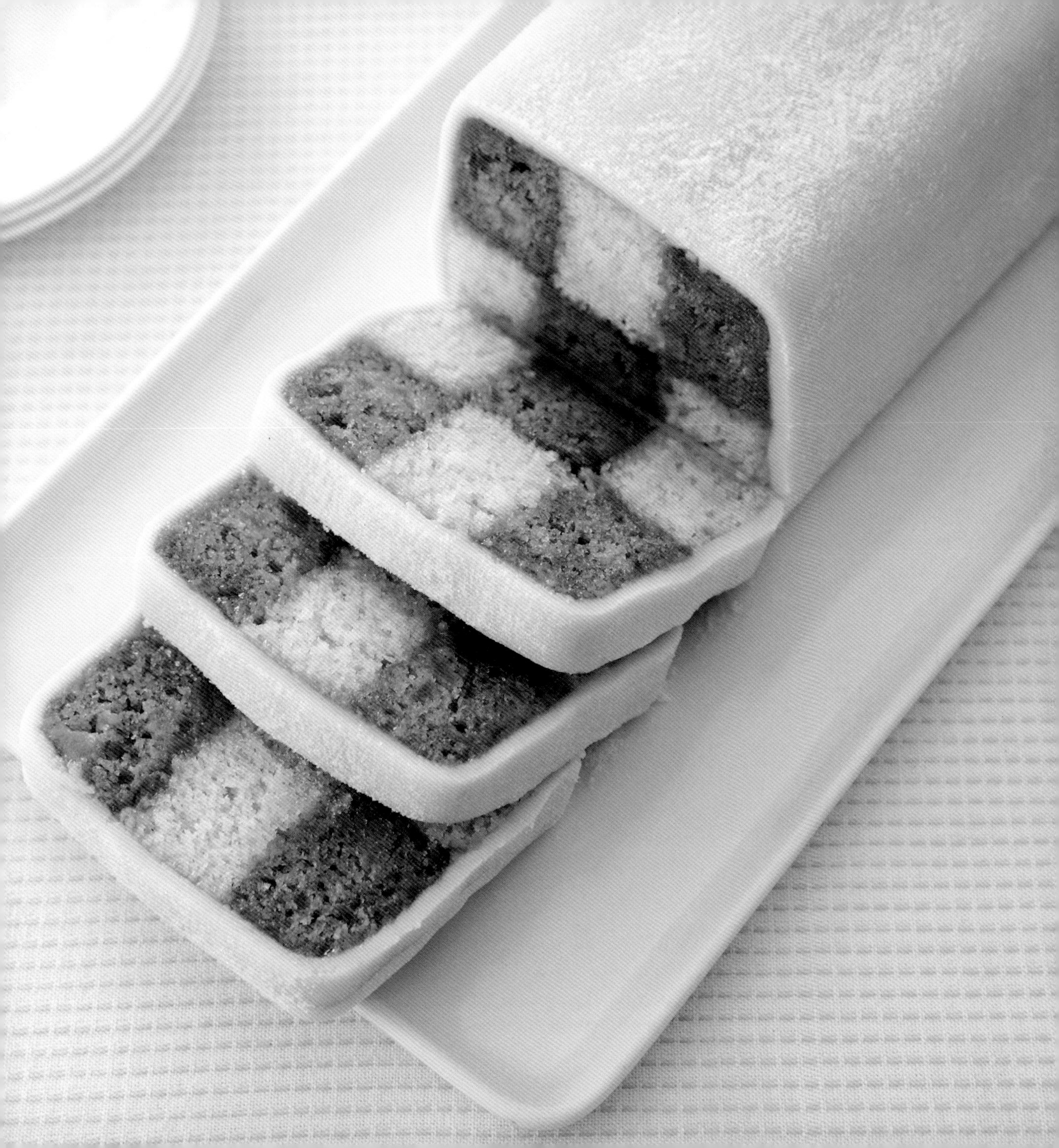

# WHITE WEDDING CAKE

~~~~~~~~~~~~~~~~~~~~~~~~~~~~

## FOR THE FIRST CAKE

7 large egg whites

½ teaspoon cream of tartar

Generous ¾ cup (175 g)
superfine sugar

2 teaspoons vanilla extract

¾ cup (100 g) all-purpose
flour

## FOR THE SECOND CAKE

2¾ sticks (325 g) slightly
salted butter, melted,
plus extra for greasing

2⅔ cups (325 g) all-purpose
flour, plus extra for
dusting

⅓ cup (40 g) unsweetened
cocoa powder

1½ teaspoons baking soda

2 cups (400 g) superfine
sugar

1 cup (150 g) finely grated
beet (about 1 small beet)

6 large eggs

⅓ cup (75 ml) whole milk

Red food coloring

## TO DECORATE

1 quantity Cream Cheese
Frosting (see page 4)

Posy of small herb flowers,
to decorate

### TO MAKE THE FIRST CAKE

Preheat the oven to 350°F (180°C). Grease and base-line an 8¼–8¾-inch (21–22-cm) square shallow baking pan (see page 7). Grease the paper. Beat the egg whites in a large, spotlessly clean bowl using an electric hand beater until foamy. Add the cream of tartar and continue to beat until the mixture forms soft peaks. Gradually add in the sugar, a tablespoonful at a time, beating well after each addition until the mixture is thick and glossy. Add the vanilla extract with the last of the sugar.

Sift the flour into the bowl and fold in gently using a large metal spoon. Turn the mixture into the pan and spread to the edges. Bake for 20–25 minutes or until just firm to the touch. Turn out onto a parchment paper-lined cooling rack, leaving the lining paper intact.

### TO MAKE THE SECOND CAKE

Grease and base-line 3 × 7-inch (18-cm) round layer pans and dust the sides with flour (see page 7). Combine the flour, cocoa powder, baking soda, and sugar in a bowl. Stir in the beet. Mix together the butter, eggs, and milk in a separate bowl and add to the mixture. Stir well and add a little red food coloring (see page 6). Divide the cake mixture evenly among the 3 cake pans. (If you only have 2 layer pans, reserve one-third of the mixture for baking separately. For accuracy, weigh the entire mixture and divide the amount by 3.)

Bake for about 30 minutes until just firm to the touch. Loosen the edges of the cakes with a knife and transfer to a cooling rack to cool.

### TO DECORATE

Peel away the paper from the first cake and cut out a 2-inch (5-cm), a 3½-inch (9-cm), and a 4½-inch (12-cm) round. Use the same 3 cutters to cut out the centers of the 3 sandwich cakes, making sure each cutter is positioned centrally before cutting. Gently press the largest white circle of cake into the center of

the largest sandwich cake, the medium-sized white circle of cake into the center of the medium-sized sandwich cake, and the smallest white circle of cake into the center of the smallest sandwich cake.

Making sure the cake with the largest white center is on the base and the cake with the smallest white center is on the top, sandwich the three cake layers together on a serving plate with a little of the cream cheese frosting. If the white cakes are shallower than the dark cakes you may need to spread a

little frosting over them so they're the same level. Transfer 5 tablespoons of the frosting to a small paper pastry bag and snip off the merest tip so the icing can be piped in small dots. Using a spatula spread the remaining frosting over the top and sides of the cake. Use the frosting in the bag to pipe dots of icing around the top and base of the cake.

Arrange a little posy of small herb flowers on top of the cake before serving, sealing the cut ends in a small piece of plastic wrap.

SERVES 12
PREPARATION AND DECORATING TIME
ABOUT 1 HOUR, PLUS COOLING

2¾ sticks (325 g) slightly
   salted butter, melted,
   plus extra for greasing

2⅔ cups (325 g) all-purpose
   flour, plus extra for
   dusting

¼ cup (25 g) unsweetened
   cocoa powder

1½ teaspoons baking soda

2 cups (400 g) superfine
   sugar

1 cup (150 g) finely grated
   beet (about 1 small beet)

6 large eggs, beaten

⅓ cup (75 ml) whole milk

Red food coloring

## TO DECORATE

1 quantity Chocolate
   Buttercream (see page 4)

About 13 oz (400 g) mixed
   candies, such as gold
   coins, candy necklaces,
   jellies, and fruit chews

Gold dragees in various
   sizes, to scatter

# TREASURE TROVE

◇◇◇◇◇◇◇◇◇◇◇◇◇◇◇◇◇◇◇◇◇◇◇◇◇◇◇◇◇◇◇◇

## TO MAKE THE CAKE

Preheat the oven to 350°F (180°C). Grease and base-line 3 × 7-inch (18-cm) round layer pans and dust the sides with flour (see page 7). Combine the flour, cocoa powder, baking soda, and sugar in a large bowl. Stir in the grated beet. Mix together the butter, eggs, and milk in a separate bowl and add to the cake mixture. Stir well and add the red food coloring (see page 6). Divide equally between the 3 cake pans. (If you only have two layer pans, reserve one-third of the batter for baking separately. For accuracy, weigh the entire mixture and divide it by three.)

Bake for 30 minutes until just firm to the touch. Loosen the edges of the cakes with a knife and transfer to a cooling rack to cool, preferably overnight, before removing the lining paper.

## TO DECORATE

Cut out the center of one of the cake layers using a 3½-inch (9-cm) round metal cutter. If you don't have a cutter, position a small bowl or container on the sponge and cut around with a knife, keeping the knife vertical. Lift out the center. (Freeze the cut-out cake for another time—see page 7.)

Press the cutter down into the other two cake layers to leave an impression, without cutting right through. Use a spoon to scoop out concave cavities from the two cakes using the marked circles as the boundary.

Place one of these cakes, concave side face up on a plate and, using a spatula, spread the edges with a little chocolate buttercream to seal in the crumbs. Position the ring cake on top. Spread the edges of this with buttercream. Pile all the candies into the cavity until completely filled and doming them up slightly in the center. (Keep any excess candies for scattering around the cake.) Position the remaining cake on top, concave side face down.

Spread a thin layer of the remaining buttercream over the top and sides of the cake to seal in the crumbs, then spread the cake with the remainder. Scatter the dragees on top to serve.

# STRIPEY **SPICE** CAKE

|||||||||||||||||||||||||||||||||||||||||||||||||||||||||||||||||||||||

## FOR THE SPICE CAKE

2 sticks (225 g) slightly salted butter, softened, plus extra for greasing

Generous 1 cup (225 g) dark brown sugar

2 teaspoons ground ginger

1 teaspoon ground cinnamon

4 large eggs, beaten

2¼ cups (275 g) self-rising flour

## FOR THE VANILLA CAKE

1½ sticks (175 g) slightly salted butter, softened

Generous ¾ cup (175 g) superfine sugar

3 large eggs, beaten

1¾ cups (225 g) self-rising flour

2 teaspoons vanilla extract

## TO DECORATE

5 tablespoons store-bought caramel sauce

1 quantity Cream Cheese Frosting (see page 4)

10–12 walnut halves

### TO MAKE THE SPICE CAKE

Preheat the oven to 325°F (160°C). Grease and line the base and side of an 8-inch (20-cm) round cake pan (see page 7). Grease the paper. Put the butter, sugar, and spices in a large bowl and beat with a wooden spoon or an electric hand beater until pale and creamy. Gradually beat in the eggs a little at a time, adding a spoonful of the flour if the mixture starts to curdle. Add the flour and fold in gently using a large metal spoon. Turn the mixture into the pan and level the surface.

Bake for 1¼ hours or until firm to the touch and a skewer inserted into the center comes out clean. Transfer to a cooling rack to cool before removing the lining paper.

### TO MAKE THE VANILLA CAKE

Grease and line the base and side of a 6-inch (15-cm) round cake pan. Grease the paper.

Put the butter and sugar in a large bowl and beat with a wooden spoon or an electric hand beater until pale and creamy. Gradually beat in the eggs a little at a time, adding a spoonful of the flour if the mixture starts to curdle. Stir in the vanilla extract. Add the flour and fold in gently using a large metal spoon. Turn the mixture into the pan and level the surface.

Bake for 1–1¼ hours or until firm to the touch and a skewer inserted into the center comes out clean. Transfer to a cooling rack to cool before removing the lining paper.

### TO DECORATE

Cut out a 6-inch (15-cm) diameter circle from a sheet of paper. Using a pencil draw a 4½-inch (12-cm) diameter circle inside, then 3¼-inch (8-cm) and 1¼-inch (3-cm) diameter circles inside this. (Use cutters to draw around.)

Place the circle of paper on top of the spice cake, making sure it is positioned centrally. Using a sharp knife cut around the circle and right down through the cake, making sure the knife is held vertically. Remove the circle of paper from the cake, cut the outer ring away from it, and then place it on top of the cake again. Cut around this smaller circle right down through the cake as before. Transfer the circle of paper to the vanilla cake and again cut around the circle right down through the cake. Cut away the next ring from the paper and cut smaller circles into the two cakes. Finally cut away the next ring from the circle of paper to leave only the 1¼-inch (3-cm) center and cut around this on both cakes.

Carefully separate all the rings of cake. Spread the cut inside edges of the outer ring of spice cake with a little caramel sauce and push the largest vanilla cake inside it. Continue to assemble the cake in this way, alternating the flavors until you end up with a circle of vanilla cake in the center. Transfer to a serving plate and freeze the cake trimmings for another time (see page 7).

Using a spatula spread the cream cheese frosting over the top and sides of the cake then decorate the top of the cake by running the tines of a fork over the frosting and arranging walnut halves around the edges.

SERVES 8–10
PREPARATION AND DECORATING TIME
ABOUT 1½ HOURS, PLUS COOLING

## FOR THE FLOWER

1⅛ sticks (125 g) slightly
   salted butter, softened,
   plus extra for greasing

Generous ½ cup (125 g)
   superfine sugar

2 large eggs

1¼ cups (150 g) self-rising
   flour

½ teaspoon baking powder

1 tablespoon whole milk

Orange and green food
   colorings

## FOR THE CAKE

1⅛ sticks (125 g) slightly
   salted butter, softened

Generous ½ cup (125 g)
   superfine sugar

Finely grated zest of 1 small
   orange

2 large eggs

1¼ cups (150 g) self-rising
   flour

½ teaspoon baking powder

2 tablespoons whole milk

## TO DECORATE

1 quantity White Chocolate
   Ganache (see page 5)

2 oz (50 g) orange ready-to-
   use icing

Confectioners' sugar, for
   dusting

Small piece green ready-to-
   use icing

# FLOWER CAKE

• • • • • • • • • • • • • • • • • • • • • • • • • • • • • • • • • • • • •

TO MAKE THE FLOWER

Preheat the oven to 325°F (160°C). Grease and line the bases and sides
of 2 × 14-oz (400-g) food cans and the base of a dariole mold (see page
7). Grease the paper. Put all the ingredients for the flower, except the food
colorings and milk, in a large bowl and beat with an electric hand beater until
pale and creamy. Stir in the milk. Transfer 2¾ oz (75 g) of the mixture to a
smaller bowl. Add orange food coloring to the mixture in the larger bowl and
green food coloring to the mixture in the smaller bowl (see page 6).

Spoon the green mixture into the dariole mold and divide the orange mixture
between the food cans. Bake the mold for 20 minutes and the food cans for
40 minutes or until a skewer inserted into the center comes out clean. Transfer
to a cooling rack to cool before removing the lining paper. Keep the oven on.

Slice the domed crusts off the orange cakes so they fit a loaf pan measuring
7 × 4½ inches (18 × 12 cm) with a depth of 3 inches (7.5 cm) when positioned
end to end. (If necessary trim off a little more cake.) Cut out their centers by
twisting an apple corer through the center of each. Cut lengths of the green
cake with the apple corer and push them down into the centers of the orange
cakes until filled. Take a flower cutter, about 2½ inches (6 cm) in diameter,
and push it down the length of each orange cake to cut the cakes into flowers.

TO MAKE THE CAKE

Grease and line the base and sides of the loaf pan. Put all the ingredients for
the cake, except the milk, in a bowl and beat until pale and creamy. Stir in the
milk. Spread 7 oz (200 g) of the cake mixture into the loaf pan. Position the
flower cakes in the pan, end to end, pushing them down into the cake mixture.

Spoon the remaining cake mixture around the flower cakes, doming it slightly
in the center so the flower cakes are thinly covered. (The mixture will rise up
during baking to cover the flower cakes even more.) Bake for about 45 minutes

or until a skewer inserted into the white cake comes out clean. Transfer to a cooling rack to cool before removing the lining paper.

TO DECORATE

Invert the cake onto a serving plate. Put the white chocolate ganache into a large pastry bag fitted with a large star tip and pipe lines along the top and sides of the cake. Roll out the orange icing on a surface dusted with confectioners' sugar and cut out small flower shapes using a cutter about ¾ inch (2 cm) in diameter. Roll tiny balls of green icing and push into the centers, securing (if they don't stay in place) with a dampened paintbrush. Arrange the flowers on top of the cake.

SERVES 14–16
PREPARATION AND DECORATING TIME
ABOUT 1¾ HOURS, PLUS COOLING

## FOR THE HALLOWEEN SHAPES

2 sticks (225 g) slightly salted butter, softened, plus extra for greasing

Generous 1 cup (225 g) superfine sugar

4 large eggs

2 cups (250 g) self-rising flour

⅓ cup (40 g) unsweetened cocoa powder

Several chocolate cookies, such as Oreos

## FOR THE CAKE

3⅛ sticks (350 g) slightly salted butter, softened

1⅔ cups (350 g) superfine sugar

2 teaspoons vanilla extract

6 large eggs, beaten

3⅔ cups (450 g) self-rising flour

Blue, yellow, and orange food coloring

## TO DECORATE

1 quantity Dark Chocolate Ganache (see page 5)

Several bought or homemade sugar or edible paper flying bats

# HALLOWEEN SCENE

### TO MAKE THE HALLOWEEN SHAPES

Preheat the oven to 325°F (160°C). Grease and line the bases and sides of two 10¼ × 7 inch (26 × 18 cm) shallow baking pans (see page 7). Grease the paper. (If you only have one pan, bake half the mixture at a time.)

Put the butter, sugar, eggs, and flour in a large bowl and beat with an electric hand beater until pale and creamy. Spoon half the mixture into one pan. Beat the cocoa into the remainder and turn the mixture into the other pan. Level the surfaces. Bake for 25 minutes or until risen and just firm to the touch. Transfer to a cooling rack to cool before removing the lining paper. Keep the oven on.

Using "ghost" and "half moon" cutters measuring 1½–2 inches (4–5cm), cut out shapes from the paler cake. (You will need about 9–10 of each shape.) Use the handle end of a fine paintbrush to press two "eye holes" through each of the ghost shapes. Slice the cookies into thin strips, each about ⅓ inch (7–8 mm) wide, and push into the eyeholes. (If the cookies are brittle and break into pieces as you slice them, pop each one in the microwave for about 10 seconds and try again. They should be soft enough to slice.)

Using "headstone" and "bat" cutters measuring 2½ inches (6 cm), cut out shapes from the chocolate cake. (You will need about 9–10 of each shape.)

### TO MAKE THE CAKE

Grease and line the base and sides of a 6-inch (15-cm) square cake pan (see page 7). Grease the paper. Put the butter, sugar, and vanilla extract in a large bowl and beat with a wooden spoon or an electric hand beater until pale and creamy. Gradually beat in the eggs a little at a time, adding a spoonful of the flour if the mixture starts to curdle. Add the flour and fold in gently using a large metal spoon until just combined. Divide the mixture between 2 bowls. Add a little blue food coloring to one bowl (see page 6). Take 2¾ oz (75 g) of the uncolored mixture and add a little yellow food coloring. Spread this into the pan. Color the remaining mixture orange. Arrange a line of the

headstone shapes across the pan, standing upright just off-center and packing them fairly tightly together. Press them down gently into the cake mixture. Pack a line of ghost shapes alongside the headstones in the same way, propping the shapes up slightly on spoonfuls of orange cake mixture. Spread the remaining orange cake mixture around the cake shapes. (The cake mixture will rise up during baking to cover the pink cakes entirely.) Bake for about 50 minutes or until a skewer inserted into the orange cake comes out clean. Transfer to a cooling rack to cool before removing the lining paper.

Wash the pan and grease and re-line it. Spread the bottom of the pan with a thin layer of blue cake mixture. Pack a line of moons along one side of the pan, propping

the shapes up slightly on one side with extra cake mixture. Do the same with a line of bats. Spread the remaining blue cake mixture around the cake shapes and bake as above. Transfer to a cooling rack to cool before removing the lining paper.

## TO DECORATE

Stack the blue cake on top of the orange cake on a serving plate, making sure the Halloween shapes are running in the same direction. Use a spatula to spread the top and sides with an even layer of dark chocolate ganache. Run the tines of a fork over the surface of the frosting to decorate. Arrange the sugar or edible paper bats on top.

# MACARON LAYER CAKE

SERVES 8
PREPARATION AND COOKING TIME
ABOUT 1 HOUR

1½ sticks (175 g) slightly salted butter, softened, plus extra for greasing

2 teaspoons instant espresso coffee granules or powder

Generous ¾ cup (175 g) superfine sugar

3 large eggs, beaten

2 cups (250 g) self-rising flour

## TO DECORATE

3–5 French macarons in various flavors, about 2½–3 inches (6–7.5 cm) in diameter

Pink, lilac, or green food coloring

½ quantity Vanilla Buttercream (see page 4)

Slivered almonds, lightly toasted, to sprinkle

## TO MAKE THE CAKE

Preheat the oven to 325°F (160°C). Grease and line the base and side of a 6-inch (15-cm) round cake pan (see page 7). Grease the paper. Blend the coffee granules with 2 teaspoons hot water.

Put the butter and sugar in a large bowl and beat with a wooden spoon or an electric hand beater until pale and creamy. Gradually beat in the eggs a little at a time, adding a spoonful of the flour if the mixture starts to curdle. Add the flour and fold in gently using a large metal spoon, adding the coffee once the flour is almost blended. Turn the mixture into the pan and level the surface.

Bake for 1–1¼ hours or until firm to the touch and a skewer inserted into the center comes out clean. Transfer to a cooling rack to cool before removing the lining paper.

## TO DECORATE

Take a round cutter that is slightly larger than the diameter of the macarons and press down into the center of the cake. (The cutter will not reach all the way through the cake.) Lift out the cut area. (Freeze all the trimmings for another time—see page 7.) Use a thin-bladed knife to cut out the remaining cake in the center, making sure you keep the knife vertical. Place the ring cake on a serving plate.

Beat a little pink, lilac, or green food coloring into the vanilla buttercream and use a spatula to spread a little onto the plate at the base of the cut-out center using a long-handled teaspoon. Press a macaron down over it. Spread with a little more buttercream, then another macaron. Continue layering up the macarons until the center of the cake is filled.

Spread the remaining buttercream over the top and sides of the cake in an even layer. Scatter the top of the cake with toasted slivered almonds.

SERVES 12
PREPARATION AND DECORATING TIME
ABOUT 1 HOUR, PLUS COOLING

2¼ sticks (250 g) slightly salted butter, softened, plus extra for greasing

2 cups (250 g) self-rising flour, plus extra for dusting

⅔ cup (40 g) shelled pistachio nuts

3 tablespoons (25 g) fresh or defrosted frozen raspberries

1¼ cups (250 g) superfine sugar

4 large eggs

1 teaspoon baking powder

Pink and green food coloring

1½ oz (40 g) white chocolate, grated

TO DECORATE

1 quantity White Chocolate Ganache (see page 5)

# PISTACHIO, RASPBERRY, AND WHITE CHOCOLATE CHECKERBOARD CAKE

||||||||||||||||||||||||||||||||||||||||||||||||||||||||||||||||

## TO MAKE THE CAKE

Grease and base-line 3 × 7-inch (18-cm) round layer pans and dust the sides with flour (see page 7). Pulse the pistachios in a food processor until finely ground. Mash the raspberries in a small bowl with a fork until pureed. Put the butter, sugar, eggs, flour, and baking powder in a large bowl and beat with an electric hand beater until smooth and creamy. Divide the mixture evenly between 3 bowls.

Beat the raspberry puree and a little pink food coloring (see page 6) into the mixture in one bowl. Beat the ground pistachios and a little green food coloring into the mixture in the second bowl. Beat the white chocolate into the mixture in the third bowl. Turn the mixture into the 3 cake pans and level the surfaces. (If you only have 2 layer pans, reserve one-third of the mixture for baking separately. For accuracy, weigh the entire mixture and divide the amount by 3.) Bake for 25 minutes or until just firm to the touch. Loosen the edges of the cakes with a knife and transfer to a cooling rack to cool before removing the lining paper.

## TO DECORATE

Position a small bowl or container with a diameter of 4½ inches (12 cm) on the center of one cake. Cut around it with a knife, keeping the knife vertical. Lift out the center and repeat on the other two cakes so you have 3 ring cakes and 3 small cakes. Use a 2½-inch (6-cm) round cutter to remove the centers of the small cakes. Reassemble all the cake pieces so each cake contains the 3 different flavors.

Using a spatula, sandwich the 3 cake layers together on a serving plate with white chocolate ganache. Spread a thin layer of ganache over the top and around the sides of the cake to seal in the crumbs. Spread the remaining ganache over the top and sides of the cake in an even layer.

SERVES 12–14

PREPARATION AND DECORATING TIME
ABOUT 1 HOUR, PLUS COOLING
AND FREEZING

2⅝ sticks (300 g) slightly
salted butter, cut into
pieces, plus extra for
greasing

2½ cups (300 g) self-rising
flour, plus extra for
dusting

1½ cups (300 g) light brown
sugar

8 oz (250 g) semisweet
chocolate, chopped

4 large eggs, beaten

2 teaspoons vanilla extract

4 tablespoons unsweetened
cocoa powder

TO DECORATE

1 quart (1 liter) tub
Neapolitan flavor
soft-scoop ice cream

1 quantity Chocolate
Meringue Frosting
(see page 5)

# NEAPOLITAN SURPRISE CAKE

## TO MAKE THE CAKE

Preheat the oven to 350°F (180°C). Grease and base-line 2 × 7-inch (18-cm) round layer pans and dust the sides with flour (see page 7). Put the butter, sugar, and chocolate in a large saucepan and heat gently, stirring frequently, until the chocolate has melted. Don't let the mixture boil. Remove from the heat once the ingredients are combined and allow to cool for 5 minutes.

Stir in the eggs and vanilla extract. Sift the flour and cocoa powder into the pan and fold in gently using a large metal spoon until combined. Divide one-half of the mixture between the two pans, spreading it to the edges. Bake for 25 minutes until just firm to the touch. Allow to cool in the pans for 10 minutes. Loosen the edges with a knife and carefully invert onto a cooling rack to cool, leaving the lining paper intact.

Wash the pans and grease and re-line them. Bake the remaining mixture in the same way. Turn each of the cakes out to cool then peel away the lining paper.

Place one cake layer on a freezerproof serving plate. Cut out the centers of 2 of the cake layers by positioning a small bowl or container with a diameter of 4½ inches (12 cm) on the centers of the cakes and cutting around with a knife, keeping the knife vertical. Lift out the centers. (Make a mini chocolate cake with these, sandwiching them with whipped cream or buttercream and dusting them with cocoa powder, or freeze for another time—see page 7.)

Carefully position the two ring cakes on top of the cake on the plate to make a shell. Freeze for a couple of hours to firm up.

## TO DECORATE

Scoop 7 oz (200 g) of the chocolate ice cream from the tub and mash it lightly to soften. Spread it into the cake shell and level the surface with the back of a spoon. Freeze for several hours until firm. Scoop 7 oz (200 g) of the vanilla ice cream from the tub and spread it over the chocolate flavor, leveling the surface.

Refreeze until firm and finish by spreading with the strawberry ice cream. Rest the remaining cake layer on top and return the cake to the freezer. Using a spatula spread the frosting all over the top and sides of the cake. Return to the freezer.

To serve, transfer the cake to the fridge for about 1 hour before slicing.

## GLOSSARY

All-purpose flour = plain flour
Apple pie spice = ground mixed
 spice
Beet = beetroot
Cake or baking pan = cake tin
Can = tin
Candies = sweets
Confectioners' sugar = icing sugar
Cookie or cracker = biscuit
Cornmeal = polenta
Dark brown sugar = dark
 muscovado sugar
Dragees = sugar balls
Electric hand beater = electric
 hand whisk
Frosting = icing
Graham crackers = digestive biscuits
Heaping = heaped
Heavy cream = double cream
Jelly = jam
Layer pan = sandwich tin
Light brown sugar = light
 muscovado sugar
Light corn syrup = golden syrup
Parchment paper = baking
 parchment
Pastry bag = piping bag
Pie weights = baking beans
Plastic wrap = cling film
Ready-to-use icing = ready-to-roll
 icing
Self-rising flour = self-raising flour
Semisweet chocolate = plain
 chocolate
Spatula = palette knife
Superfine sugar = caster sugar
Piping tip = piping nozzle
Vanilla bean = vanilla pod
Wax paper = greaseproof paper

## CONVERSIONS

1 teaspoon = 5 ml
1 tablespoon = 15 ml

Where eggs are used US sizing
is described. A US large egg is the
equivalent to a UK medium egg.

For those who cook with gas, the
temperature conversion you will
require when baking the basic
cake recipe is:

325°F/160°C/Gas Mark 3
350°F/180°C/Gas Mark 4